CHARLES E. SMITH, PhD

NAVIGATING FROM THE FUTURE

A PRIMER FOR SUSTAINABLE TRANSFORMATION

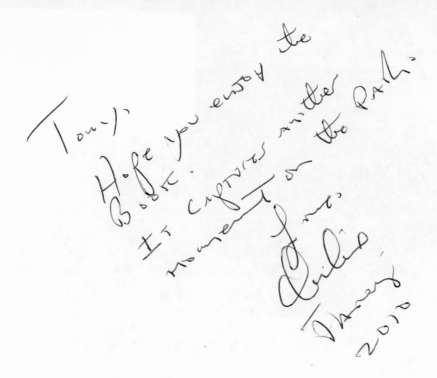

To [illegible],
Hope you enjoy the
Book. It captures another
moment on the path.
Love,
[signature]
January
2010

ISBN: 1-4392-3793-X
ISBN-13: 9781439237939

www.Booksurge.com

Cover Art:	Velka Edge-Olok, www.FirstArtOnTheMoon.com
Cover Concept:	Matt Asinari, www.m2brandStudios.com
Cover Design:	Roger Bentley, www.RogerBentley.com
Fine Art Photo:	D. James Dee, www.theSohoPhotographer.com
Portrait Photo:	Meaghan Smith, www.peacelovephotography.com

Visit *NavigatingFromTheFuture.com* to purchase books, contact the author, and learn more about this work.

ACKNOWLEDGEMENTS

I thank my teachers for their examples:

Werner Erhard for demonstrating that power comes from context.
Robert Mirabal, for teaching that everything is alive.
Dick Beckhard, for the need to balance order and creativity.
Lew Epstein, for showing that a person can learn compassion.
Ron Bynum, for the ability to be strong with good humor.
Neil Mahoney, for how to be free from being victim of circumstance.
Jonathan Smith, for taking our ideas farther than I'd ever imagined.
Michael Smith, for the example of creativity unleashed.
Marilyn Smith, for my best example of self-control and love.
Meaghan Smith, for the possibility of integrating beauty, the good and the true.
Marcia Smith, for the ability to climb a mountain that has no top.
Susan Smith, for bringing me a perfect balance of rigor and affection.
Mick Crews, for his constant support and friendship, whatever I do.
Frank Hennessey, for teaching me to respect political and social views I don't like.
Erving Polster, for showing that integrating madness and accuracy keeps one alive.
Lee J. Dunn, for giving me the opportunity for a fine education.
Michael Jordan, for proving that only you can do it, but you can't do it alone.
I also want to thank Kathy Smith for knowing what I want to say and what I should say. Her support in encouraging this book, editing, and commentary was invaluable.

.

TABLE OF CONTENTS

Upon a small number of committed, humane people,
    the future of the world depends
Radical departures are impossible where we most need them
Transformation is always possible; a few will show the way
Organizations with the most available energy will prevail

PREFACE

Navigating From the Future is a self-help book that is not trying to help, but rather, to tell the truth about what it takes to make transformation happen *and sustain it.* It is written with great optimism and pessimism at the same time. The optimism comes from long experience that says transformation is always possible. The pessimism comes from the fact that most people and organizations are always living in a condition of *No Exit*.

In Jean Paul Sartre's *No Exit*, three people are escorted into a room, where they create their own hell. When one finally demands for the door to be opened (it was never locked, only closed), the door opens, yet none of them leave.

No Exit is common in most corporate, government,
and community hierarchies.

No Exit exists in most religions and tribes.

No Exit prevails in just about anything that involves people.

No Exit eventually undermines every business, political,
economic, and spiritual system.

No Exit is the impossibility of transformation.

Transformation is a change in composition or structure, a change in character or condition. Transformation is a new possibility, a "wow" that promises more. Transformation is what makes people jump out of bed in the morning and move into their day with enthusiasm and energy. It is the opportunity to start anew or re-vitalize what already exists.

Sustainability normally means keeping a prior innovation alive. The power of transformation, however, comes with returning to a zero state – the place of creativity and invention. It involves a new and free choice to breathe life into what you already have, or to choose a new direction. Trying to keep an old choice going does not work. Recent research from an inventive, global computer chip corporation showed that ninety percent of innovation projects do not sustain. The reasons lie in all of the cultural, technical, and personal mental baggage that has accumulated. To achieve *Sustainable Transformation*, you have to repeatedly access that empty place in the mind where free choice lives – the Moment of Change.

Many people will say they want transformation at work, in government, at home, and in the world, but few demonstrate the courage, talent, and concern for others necessary to become transformational leaders. This is not a criticism. It's just the way it is. Most of us are ordinary human beings, doing what we do.

My hope is that telling my own truth will set more people free to navigate from the future. Telling our own truth is the code breaker in all human affairs — business, public, and private. It is the transformational element.

It's simple, not easy.

Charles E. Smith, PhD
July 2009

*Upon a small number of committed,
humane people, the future
of the world depends.*

This book is about the power of imagination and
"thinking outside the box" to produce radical
breakthroughs and collective innovation.

Frank O'Connor, the Irish poet, wrote that as a boy, he and his friends would wander through the fields, and when they came to a high stone wall, they would throw their hats over that wall and then had no choice but to follow.[1]

Through forty years of change management consulting and training, I have met only a few people willing to do this. The "wall" is always a fear rooted in deep concern about some aspect of their company, agency, community, nation, or their own lives. When they throw their hats over that wall, and take on an ambitious challenge in the face of these concerns, the imagination and the commitments described in this book come alive.

Grounded in these people's courage, clarity, and talent, transformational business success and values-based social transformation always follow from the inevitable capturing of other people's hearts and minds. Thinking becomes a collective phenomenon. Our common humanity becomes the container for business and social commitments.

These people are *navigators*.

Navigators help others do what they are capable of, not just what they would do anyway. I have met a number of such leaders,

---

1   *The Best of Frank O'Connor*, Everyman's Library, Frank O'Connor and Julian Barnes, 2009

facilitators, engineers, managers, lawyers, and educators. There are many more — either in hiding, staying out of the limelight, or just not knowing what is possible.

In business, government, and communities, we have become so specialized that we can't easily talk about and influence each other's approaches to our jobs and lives without a very special effort to do so. This special effort doesn't happen often because people are locked up in their fundamental points of view — the mental paradigms that shape what they are able to see and listen to, and that stop the possibility of collective action dead in its tracks.

RADICAL DEPARTURES ARE IMPOSSIBLE WHERE WE MOST NEED THEM

The paradigm for some is the necessity for sound engineering and scientific analysis before constructive conversation is allowed. For others, spiritual consciousness and a bottom line of caring for people is pivotal. The paradigm for some is the necessity for an a priori, well-financed institutional framework. For others, the paradigm is a need for sound policy formulation before anything meaningful can happen. For still others, it is the necessity for senior political support. For some, it is profit.

The outcome of all this paradigm paralysis is that this brilliant energy never gets focused collectively. Instead, endless conversations take place, trying to satisfy individual paradigm interests. New technologies for inexpensive energy independence, clean environments, and social transformation either can't move forward or don't develop fast enough to make a difference.

Recently I was in an e-mail conversation with a group of scientists, engineers, lawyers, and businesspeople about "the future of space" efforts in the United States. One man said:

You are all correct in your comments. But, how can this team make a difference and help to improve the situation? We are only preaching to each other and venting our frustrations concerning perceived problems.

He asked the group:

Does anyone have a viable game plan to help implement needed changes at the various levels needed throughout the aerospace industrial, governmental, and academic communities?

Does anyone have recommendations for fixing our space program-related research, development, test, and operational control issues?

Does anyone have proposals regarding the need for clear-cut life-cycle cost estimating and control techniques to establish and maintain critical budget and schedule requirements?

He concluded:

Business leaders, engineers, scientists, financial managers, political scientists, lawyers, program/project managers, sociologists, and bureaucracy analysts do not normally communicate well with each other. By facilitating dialogue to help them become aware of and sensitive to the operating principles/requirements unique to each discipline, we can help avoid time-critical or financial-budget project killers.

This is a perfect demonstration of a place where dialogue is blocked and the opposite needs to be true. The military seems only able to find shared meaning with the military. NASA only seems able to hear NASA. Educators only seem able to hear other educators. Engineers only hear engineers, etc.

Paradigms talk to themselves. Unless someone finds a way to start and sustain meaningful dialogue across parts of the system, this will stay in a past-based vicious circle. In the space context, this "moth to the flame" production of more and more scientific, procedural, and engineering recommendations is like winking in the dark.

Blocking all conversations except dialogue frees imagination. Nothing else will work. Otherwise, left to our own purposes, people will inform, debate, tell, expound, opine, and operate from their own realities. Dialogue is the only form of shared reality that will get us there.

If I were king, I'd forbid every kind of talk except for dialogue, for at least twenty hours out of every day. Only dialogue —open-ended, mutual, vulnerable conversation — leads to shared meaning. Without dialogue, people either don't listen or never change their minds, paradigms, or points of view. Without dialogue, we avoid or disparage other disciplines for not getting it right.

David Bohm said,

A new kind of mind comes into being, based on the development of a common meaning that is constantly transforming in the process of the dialogue.[2]

---

2   David Bohm, *On Dialogue*, Routledge Classics Series, 2004; Vol.I

Without shared meaning, there is little collective action or shared commitment.

Without shared meaning, we go our own ways or become superficial with people who are not like us.

Without shared meaning, we drop out mentally and stay in familiar gardens.

TRANSFORMATION IS ALWAYS POSSIBLE;
A FEW WILL SHOW THE WAY

Entrepreneurial spirit, cooperation, and breakthroughs that benefit all are always possible. The missing ingredient is always transformational or moral leadership.

Miracles happen when leaders commit to incredible goals, like Peter H. Diamandis' X Prize Foundation's mission, *to bring about radical breakthroughs for the benefit of humanity,* with prizes for successful accomplishment, such as ten million dollars for a suborbital commercially sponsored space flight.

Making the case for this with a lot of corporate and public examples rarely makes a difference. Taking this on is not first a matter of evidence. The men and women I've seen, in corporations and government agencies who have taken on such radical departures did not need to be convinced.

> Leaders without the potential for "throwing their
> hats over the wall" *will not* be convinced.
> They have to first believe it to see it.

The point of this book is the realization that incredible goals and collective innovation have become more important to our survival than being right about what we already know.

Through the past fifty years, organization and human resource development theory and practice have produced thousands of techniques, tips, improved processes, and better systems — none of which has made a lasting difference. The CEO of a major energy company said recently that his people were sick and tired of process, and he couldn't bear asking them to do another.

This book is about what leaders, facilitators, and consultants need to *believe* to bring about business and social transformation. It is not about teaching people to believe these things. In my view, they have to already believe them, or at least wish that they could.

From the perspective of the Navigator Code, we can see a revolutionary way of looking at organizations – perhaps even a new distinction for organization itself.

ORGANIZATIONS WITH THE MOST
AVAILABLE ENERGY WILL PREVAIL

Simply, I'm asking you to consider the possibility that an organization can be viewed *completely* as interacting energy fields, rather than as physical objects, people, materials, or even processes and procedures. From this perspective it is inevitable that organizations with the most available energy *will* prevail.

This point of view began for me when I met a Pomo Indian medicine man named Lorin Smith. He said that, for his people, all of life is about maintaining, preserving, and increasing energy. He said that what's most missing and most needed in the world at large is paying extraordinary attention to energy, vitality, and the power to act.

Energy is everywhere, and when an individual or a group is in harmony with it, life works. When energy or vitality is ignored, life doesn't fulfill its promise.

As Lorin spoke, it struck me that in business, leadership has a lot to do with getting energy to the places it's needed. I saw that in most of the companies and government agencies I'd known, aliveness, energy, and vitality were rare. I'd see it in a hot project, a great relationship, or an exciting start-up. But for the most part, the people I met were not animated and had elaborate explanations for their difficult circumstances.

The next step in my transition from a static to an energetic-based point of view occurred when I studied with Victor Sanchez, who had lived with Toltec Indians in northern Mexico. A scholar as well as a teacher, Victor introduced me to the Toltec belief that the world does not consist of objects, but rather of interacting energy fields, and that the systems with the greatest available energy will prevail. Good ideas and the force of will are not enough.[3]

This fit with my own experience. Relationships with the most vitality seem to be ones that thrive. People with money and power usually prevail over people without them.

In a successful revolution, the disenfranchised gather their collective energy, which becomes greater than that of the establishment, and thus prevail. (This can easily be seen in both the Russian Revolution and the American Civil Rights Movement.)

---

3   *The Teachings of Don Carlos: Practical Applications of the Works of Carlos Castaneda*, Victor Sanchez, Bear and Company, 1995

Albert Einstein said we should *make everything as simple as possible, but not simpler.* Let's say that success equals energy (S = E), and that success is the achievement of a measurable goal, while energy is measured by people's subjective assessment of their "power to act." It is then "the power to act" that determines success.

Everywhere that I've seen results-producing personal or organizational transformation — in industry, government, or even in families — it's been accompanied by an increase in people's or a group's sense of their own power to act. In situations where physical resources were taken away or market conditions changed, the outcomes were *still* a function of the impact of those changes on people's sense of their power to act.

There are many practices, tools, and behaviors that increase this human energy. These can be invented on the spot, if that is your intent. Red Auerbach, legendary coach of the Boston Celtics basketball team, said that his main job was to assure team spirit. When team spirit went down, he went to work. Otherwise, the players were talented and did the rest themselves.

This energetic view of organizations is a radical departure from current and historical views of organizations, framed by a world view that physical and human resources are primary. This energetic perspective enables facing the many challenges before us with greater power and effect, whether we are focusing on energy independence, corporate growth, governance, innovation, national security, environmental protection, or human rights.

At the same time, it is worth noting that energy alone is amoral — in and of itself energy is neither positively nor negatively directed. In every circumstance, we are still called to address ethical dilemmas that challenge our commitments.

ARE YOU A NAVIGATOR?

Cooperation is the cork in our human bottle.

In 1964, Benjamin Bloom created a taxonomy of levels of thinking.[4] His six levels are:

Knowledge: Recall of something encountered before but without having to change it, use it, or understand it; facts.

Comprehension: Understanding the knowledge that has been acquired without needing to relate it to other information.

Application: Use of a learned concept to resolve some situation or solve a new problem in an appropriate way.

Analysis: Taking something learned apart into separate components for purposes of thinking about the parts and how they fit together.

Evaluation: Looking at the particular value of materials, information, or methods in characterizing the whole.

Synthesis: Generating or creating something different by assembling or connecting ideas in a way that makes a whole.

Understanding Bloom's levels of thinking, however, has not made much of a dent in the state of cooperation across paradigms and among conflicting interests within companies, government

---

4   *Taxonomy of Educational Objectives*, Benjamin S. Bloom, Bertram B. Mesia, and David R. Krathwohl, David McKay, New York, 1964

agencies, communities, and nations. Building on this taxonomy, I assert that there is another level of thinking available that gives access to cooperation in otherwise unbridgeable and intractable problems that have been created at these prior levels. This new level of thinking is:

Navigation: Thinking from a future that inspires others with a sense of what's possible and helping people focus on what they are capable of, rather than just what they do.

ᏋᏋ

Our sole responsibility is to produce something smarter than we are; any problems beyond that are not ours to solve... There are no hard problems, only problems that are hard to a certain level of intelligence. Move the smallest bit upwards in level of intelligence and some problems will suddenly move from 'impossible' to 'obvious.' Move a substantial degree upwards, and all of them will become obvious.

Eliezer S. Yudkowski,
Staring into the Singularity, 1996

In the *Dune* novels by Frank Herbert, *navigators* were people who became able to safely guide others across interstellar space using a limited form of the ability to think, see, and act from the future.

They were able to see what others couldn't.

They cast their minds into the future, imagining it as if it were the present, seeing a kaleidoscope of adjacent possibilities and how to move from one to another at will.

Navigators become more and more capable through extensive exposure to paradox and multiple realities beyond their own immediate experience. As they become better able to see sets of adjacent possibilities, they become better able to help others navigate among these different possible realities and safely arrive at their desired future destinations.

A *navigator's* impossible promise is to be personally responsible for having people from different paradigms listen to one another and work together for the good of all.

Ultimately, a *navigator* stands as a bridge between others. A *navigator* can be tough, soft, direct, or political. It's a matter of paying equal attention to noble purpose and pragmatic purpose, technology and performance, team and individual spirit, relationship and measurement, physical reality and emotional reality.

A *navigator* is a human bridge between different points of view, past and future, what is and what could be.

A *navigator* does not need agreement from others to play this role — it is a calling, not a job.

A *navigator* does not operate in the ever-present worlds of right/wrong, win/lose, and "avoid the domination" of others. In the *navigator* context, people gain confidence and become able to listen generously to other points of view, with deep appreciation for the feelings and experiences of others.

Navigators think and experience in a way that enables others to work together toward collective innovation and general accomplishment.

GETTING PAST THE CRISIS

Recently, someone referred to the relationship between a major US government agency and the business and advocacy organizations it relates to as a "suicide pact." Whatever anybody says, others disagree.

We are in the midst of a crisis of cooperation, in the United States and throughout the world. Without a transformation in the way we listen to one another, humanity will self-destruct.

David Brooks wrote with resignation in the *New York Times* (July 6, 2007):

Nothing is sadder than the waning dream of integration. This dream has illuminated American life for the past several decades — the belief that the world is getting smaller and that different peoples would come together... The trauma of Sept. 11 promised to heal the rifts between red and blue America... Then there were the integrating forces of globalization and technology... The growing movement of people would pave the way for multicultural societies. The movement of goods would increase interdependence. The revolution in communications technology would increase global conversation. All these promises hung in the air, but then crumbled.

It's as though non-cooperation has been ordained and accepted as "business as usual," and part of the fabric of life.

Corporate and government bureaucracies inhibit shared reality and suppress creativity. People's experiences are shaped by the demands of their jobs, their rewards, and their aspirations. The awful truth is that most people operate in "silos" and cooperation among them is interest-based. Without immediate and apparent self-interest, cooperation doesn't happen, even within internal systems.

As a result, energy flows to the overall purpose and mission in segmented, superficial, and dissociated ways. Total system performance is suppressed because people literally don't see cooperative solutions as their primary path. Ultimately this does not serve customers or constituents. But, like most self-destructive human behavior, this is consistent and persistent.

Today's popular news media loves trouble. Early in my career, while working as a photojournalist, I did a story about a news department at a local television station. They told me they were connected to the local fire department's communication center. When there was a fire, the department would indicate whether there was smoke, or smoke and flames, and whether the flames were visible. The station would send a team to cover the fire *only* if there was an exciting amount of flame. I began to question what business they were really in.

In the same vein, I was once asked to mediate a dispute between teachers, school administrators, Board of Education members, and labor union leaders that was being videotaped for later screening by a local public television station. I did well, and it wasn't long before people were communicating, resolving some differences, and finding common ground.

During a break, the producer called me aside and said that the action was boring and could I please *stir it up and get some sparks to fly?* I did that, and people began to argue and become emotional. It was deemed a great program. The TV station was happy, and each participant ended feeling self-righteous about his or her original point of view. From a commitment to entertain, cooperation is boring.

⚭

Standardization does violence to cooperation — visible in education as the tension between schools and parents, teachers and parents, parents and children, educational style and content versus what it might mean for individual children to follow their own bliss.

Standardization and measurement seem to have become more important than education. As well-intentioned and talented as any particular teachers may be, they must operate in a context of standardization. The ills of bureaucracy have come home to our children.

The necessities, justifications, and financial arguments for this are apparent — not enough money, not enough good teachers, too many students. The case can also be made that many parents are not really committed to the nature and quality of their children's education, and therefore, the state needs to do it. None of these explanations improves the situation.

NAVIGATING FROM THE FUTURE

Paul March of Barrios Technology shared this view via email:

In today's world, navigators *see where we want to be led and how to go about it, such that our actions will deliver our goals — maximizing individual freedoms, self-discipline, self-worth and fulfillment, while maximizing individual return to the human family. This is a journey of self-discovery, accomplishment, and a search for ultimate meaning.*

March sees *navigators* as:

Men and women who think from the future, live by a code, and train themselves to see what others don't see. They come from every walk of life, people at every level of community, business and science. A navigator *leads and has the tools needed to do this successfully.*

They seek numbers of imagined universes, allowing individuals to excel, creating economic and social systems based on unlimited, non-polluting energy that increases the lowest income levels up to the equivalent of today's upper middle class or higher.

He suggests that:

Navigators *seek a new social paradigm which encourages design and development of technologies that create a new universe of plenty. And that will only happen when energy is cheaper than air.*

March concludes with:

Our question now is, how do we bootstrap ourselves to a point where the collective good can create the investments needed in energy production technologies to make this happen? Where do we start this circular logic into self-sustaining oscillation that won't dam out, but also won't self-destruct in a blaze of glory?

RADICAL DEPARTURES

Brilliant young man that he is, Jonathan Smith navigates from the future. He thinks by putting things together that never were. He takes possibilities from books or film, imagines they are real, and then spends time thinking about how they would actually work. He does this with politics, nanotechnology, social systems, and business. While he fully accepts the possibility that any of his thought experiments might seem crazy, he says, *That's the whole point —* anything *is possible!* Jonathan does not rely upon agreement for the possibilities he imagines.

John F. Kennedy thought from the future when he said we would go to the moon. I thought from the future when I said that my children would excel. Mohandas Gandhi thought from the future when he declared that India would separate from England. Thomas Jefferson thought from the future when he wrote, *These states are and [have] a right to be free.* Barack Obama thought from the future when he proposed that we could become one undivided country again.

Thinking from the future starts where there is technically nothing going on. The future is unwritten, and as much as these others, Jonathan is writing the future for himself. It begins in his mind and in the freedom he feels in being that way. There is no way I can tell how he does this. Somehow he is able to have a free play of imagination and put things together that have never been together in my experience. *Navigating from the future* is the ultimate freedom.., a gift.

Merlin, King Arthur's mentor and counselor, did not need to imagine. As given by T.H. White in *The Once and Future King*[5], Merlin had an uncanny ability to already know the future. On one occasion, he gave young Arthur insight into how he knew what was going to happen before it did:

Ah, yes, Merlin said. How did I know to set breakfast for two? Now ordinary people are born forwards in time, if you understand what I mean, and nearly everything in the world goes forward, too. This makes it quite easy for ordinary people to live. But unfortunately, I was born at the wrong end of time, and I have to live backwards from in front, while surrounded by a lot of people living forward from behind...

Albert Einstein wrote (in an unpublished personal letter shared by my friend Howard Sherman) that he'd discovered the code breaker in all human endeavors. It was that *there is no necessary relationship between sense experience and thinking.*

In other words, when we see or hear or feel something, whatever we think as a result is purely arbitrary — literally made up, based on what we already know, think is real and true, or have been told.

---

5   HarperCollins, Canada, 1997

Einstein went on to say that when we really see that our thoughts are arbitrary, that they are only there because we are making some causal necessary relationship between the thought and the action, it allows for the free play of imagination — and *that* is what allowed him to think of space and time being the same, and that they bent gravity. There was no prior basis for that thought, only bits of evidence that seemed inconsistent.

What if freedom flows from that ability? Not that I would forget where the door was and be unable to get out of the room. But, what would become possible in my life and work? In the brief moment of thinking that — and seeing that I *could* think it — I experienced the free play of imagination, and the power of it.

Imagination is (1) the faculty of imagining, or of forming mental images or concepts of what is not actually present to the senses, and (2) the action or process of forming such images or concepts.

It helps provide meaning to experience and <u>understanding</u> to knowledge; it is a fundamental facility through which people "make sense" of the world. Imagination is the faculty through which we encounter everything — the things that we touch, see, and hear, coalescing into a "picture" via our imagination.

It is the ability to problem-solve, to see things from a different perspective.

THE ABILITY TO IMAGINE

Technically, the future has nothing in it. We have never seen the future, and we never will. Even when we bring the past forward, all we see is now, now, and now.

As we think about the future right now, it is either an extension of what we already know or have seen in the past; an expression of our beliefs, commitments, or fears; or a blur we can ignore in favor of what's happening right now.

You can put anything into the future that you want to put there. People do it all the time. They put money in the future, or an afterlife, or gloom and doom. People put high taxes into the future, or great benefits, or happy retirement, or whatever. The future is a canvas onto which you can paint anything.

On one hand, this is an optimistic view that says we can create the future we want. On the other hand, it feels like a fool's errand when the weight and gravity of the past seems to keep going on in spite of our best efforts.

Still, Serge Kahili King's *The world is what we think it is*[6] seems operationally true. Isn't your world what you think it is? While you might appreciate that it may not really be that way in fact, it sure is that way for you, and you are all you've got when it comes to actually doing anything. So, if as a practical matter the world is what

---

6   *The Urban Shaman*, Simon and Schuster, 1990

you think it is, wouldn't it be nice to have the best possible ability to imagine?

In *The Brain that Changes Itself,*[7] Norman Doidge, MD, offers evidence that we can change our brain anatomy by using our imaginations. He presents experiments in which one group learned to play the piano and another group *imagined* learning to play the piano, using pictures of piano keys and the same pages of music. Identical changes were measured in the brains of each group and after both periods of practice. The imagining group, after a short time, was able to play the piano as well as the practicing group.

Referring to another experiment, he relates that when one group lifted weights in a disciplined way and another imagined lifting weights for a similar time, the actual weight lifters gained 30 percent in their muscle mass in their arms. The group imagining it gained 22 percent in muscle mass! While this is hard to conceive, it is evidence of the fact that imagination is connected to the possibility of action in a very direct way. In each case, they were able to measure the neuron activity in people's brains, demonstrating this connection.

He goes on to tell us of another experiment, in which people were subjected to extreme darkness for a long time, during which their senses of smell and hearing became vastly more acute, as is often reported happening with blind people. He offers this as evidence that the human brain can reorganize quickly because individual

---

7   Viking Books, 2007

parts of the brain are not particularly committed to processing particular senses. One part of the brain can take over for another if it's trained to do so.

What if people could learn to stop acting out Rita Mae Brown's definition of insanity — *doing the same thing over and over, expecting a different result?*

What if people *could* learn to cooperate? What if people's "stay or leave" marriages could always have a happy ending? What if we could have governance that really works for everybody? Or new and unthinkable forms of organization that provide wealth *and* are socially responsible?

We all know that human nature, the intractable identity of organizations, and the fact that power and greed too often trump virtue make all of the above seem impossible. But what if we could imagine ways that these *are* possible and act on them?

OBSTACLES TO IMAGINATION — THINKING INSIDE THE BOX

*We will start thinking out of the box when
the box is empty.*[8]

Many of us are always looking for gold at the end of the tunnel and never finding it. Maybe it's a relationship that doesn't satisfy. Maybe it's a client with whom the work is unsuccessful because he or she keeps changing the rules of the game. Maybe it's a conversation with your child or spouse that never concludes. Maybe it's a dissatisfying job that's inconsistent with the consuming passion of your life. Maybe it's that you never really do lose weight, or make the money you want.

*Instead of results, you're left with a never-ending story.
The costs are resignation, lost energy, and lack of
real contact and intensity in relationships.*

As a child it's hard to say *no* to your parents. This can become habit-forming, to the point where you stop saying *no* in situations where you easily should. By *no* I mean, *No, absolutely!* Until you say *no* there can be no possibility of a *yes* to something else.

The ability to imagine goes to hell when you can't say *no*. Not being able to say *no* keeps you stuck where you are, and anything else becomes unthinkable — not bad, just unthinkable.

---

8   a Robert Mankoff cartoon, *The New Yorker*, May 9, 2005

On the day you start saying an absolute *no* to what you don't want, you will *stop* getting more of what you don't want, and become able to start imagining what it is that you *do* want from the future — as a person, as a team, as a business.

Martin Luther King said *no* to the white establishment. Lincoln said *no* to slavery. The ability to say the final *no* to what you don't want *precedes* the ability to imagine — *precedes* navigating from the future.

PEOPLE DON'T THINK ABOUT WHAT THEY ARE PAID NOT TO THINK ABOUT

Getting paid *not to think about* something is the same as getting paid to say *yes*. It is as damaging to one's ability to imagine as not being able to say *no*. A negotiator for an arms manufacturer gets paid not to think about peaceful ways of resolving disputes. Government contractors get paid not to think about the merits of what contrary political views might suggest. Liberal TV station spokesmen get paid not to think about the merits of economic conservatism. Engineers get paid not to think nonlinearly. Scientists are paid not to stop asking questions. Academics are paid not to sound stupid. All of them are paid not to think outside whatever paradigm that's paying them, so with rare exceptions, they don't.

If you raise the subject of diversity at one UK accounting firm populated almost entirely with white males, the conversation lasts a few minutes and disappears slowly in a slough of disinterest. It's like being surrounded by Pavlovian dogs that salivate on cue.

People get paid to use language that keeps those in power in power and the identity of their organizations intact. The US auto industry recently sought a government bailout for not thinking from the future of energy, for having only thought about what was consistent with the language, character, and culture of the powers that had been in charge.

Not thinking about what you are paid to not think about kills one's ability to imagine. Inside these constraints, imagination occurs only in narrow bands, the possibility of imagination is trivialized, and navigating from a better future outside of the payment scheme is impossible.

NEVER HAVE I MET ANYONE WHO DOES NOT LIVE IN A BOX

While studying at the New York Film Academy, my son Michael made a film about a young girl who lived in a cardboard box, down an alley off a city street. She was pretty and well kept, and decorated the box with trinkets and cloth that she found on the street. She was kind to the people she met walking about, and as poor as she was, she returned a man's dropped wallet (although she did keep a few dollars for herself).

While this girl lived in a box literally, she reminded me of the rest of us who live equally in boxes without realizing it. It may be that she stopped, at a point, paying much attention to the box she lived in, as do most people. We work; we survive; we love. We look forward to the future and are wily enough to take care of ourselves, one way or another. We all live in a box, cardboard or otherwise.

There is a world outside the box, but we never see it. Inside seems like reality, not just our senses reflecting the world on the surfaces and in the depth of our imagination.

THE BOX HAS MANY WALLS, INVISIBLE BUT ALWAYS THERE

I see the boxes others live in, but not so clearly my own. Nature or nurture...where does the box come from? It's hard to say. Regardless, marriages, companies, governments, and communities crumble like cookies through inattention to boxes that suppress their imagination and vitality.

Freedom is the ability to move from the experience of being the effect of circumstances to the experience of being the cause of them, from having the mood you want and not the mood that comes from finding yourself a victim.

Freedom is the ability to get outside the box. It is not the same as liberty. Some people in concentration camps reported experiencing freedom though they did not have liberty. Freedom is the ability to imagine, and it is *always* outside the box. The spirit of such freedom can be seen in Maya Angelou's 1969 autobiography, *I Know Why the Caged Bird Sings.*

The greatness of America has always resided in its myth of possibility — that anyone can transcend what holds them back. The first step is the hardest. Most walls of the box that suppress your imagination (and the imagination and freedom of your organization) are 100 percent in you, and in each of us.

NEEDING TO BE RIGHT IS A BOX THAT
STIFLES THE ABILITY TO IMAGINE

Nobody wants to be wrong. There is a point, however, at which the need to be right becomes a wall that stifles the ability to imagine. I'm reminded of two colleagues, one a lawyer and teacher, and the other a former high government official. When I ask either of them a question, their answers are clear, direct, and reduce complexity into coherent and helpful arguments.

If, however, I offer them a plan, an idea, or a proposition to consider, they always find as many reasons as it takes to prove that it won't work. Their tone changes from helpful to one of *no possibility* and becomes something I want to flee. They move from offering intelligence in my service to intelligence that is righteous. Their "being right" gets associated with what is terribly wrong with my idea. This always happens with them, and since observing it, I now notice the same mechanism in more and more people.

This happens with any form of fundamentalism or addiction. Hard-bitten liberals can't imagine the benefits of economic conservatism. Extreme social conservatives can't imagine that liberals could be decent people. Religious fundamentalists will only imagine what their God or church culture says it's acceptable to imagine. Americans often can't imagine that many people in other countries feel just as free as they do and have lives of equal or greater quality.

The need to be right and to avoid being wrong is in our blood. It prevents navigating from the future, if the prospect might have us be wrong about what we already believe.

When leadership has to be right about what they already think, industries often don't adapt fast enough. Businesses and marriages fall apart because one or both parties have to be more right than their partner.

> *The need to be right about*
> *what you already think is real and true*
> *stops the free play of imagination.*

❦

THE PRICE OF ARROGANCE

At the beginning of everything is the word. It is a miracle to which we owe the fact that we are human. But at the same time it is a pitfall and a test, a snare and a trial. More so, perhaps, than it might appear to you who have enormous freedom of speech, and might therefore assume that words are not so important. They are. They are important everywhere. The same word can be humble at one moment and arrogant the next.

It is not hard to demonstrate that all the main threats confronting the world today, from atomic war and ecological disaster, to a catastrophic collapse of society and civilization, have hidden deep within them a single root cause: the imperceptible transformation of what was originally a humble message into an arrogant one.

Having learned from all this, we should all fight together against arrogant words and keep a weather eye out for any insidious germs of arrogance in words that are seemingly humble. Obviously this is not just a linguistic task. Responsibility for and toward words is a taste which is intrinsically ethical.

Vaclav Havel, former president of Czechoslovakia
(written from prison, between 1979 and 1982)

DOMAIN ADDICTION IS A BOX

A Managing Partner I know at a large law firm is a process addict. He seems to "mainline" procedures, forms, processes, and tools. When he came to understand that relationships were important, he started to pay attention to the mechanics of his relationships. But people's experience of connection with him, and their felt permission to form expressive relationships with others in the firm, changed not a whit. He continues to be unable to talk about or think about vision, possibilities, quantum leaps, or compassionate listening because they are not processes. If it's not a process, it isn't real for him.

Government agencies are process addicted. Many (maybe most) corporations are process addicted. It's not that effective process is considered the footprint of a commitment. Simply put, so long as it's a process, it is legitimate. Imagination is allowed so long as it's in service of process. The problem is that processes are only one part of reality.

The owners of a local sports team are content addicts. If a subject is not in the nature of content — physical objects and events — they pay no attention and their eyes glass over. They have no way to deal with disputes or the gap between what is and what might be.

An eminent scientist I know is a content addict. He is a superb analyst of physical reality. While he has profound *conceptual appreciation* for the importance of managing team spirit, energy, and having people in the same boat, he is unable to act on his insight. He lives only in the physical universe, and his appreciation of the relational universe means little because he does not live there. Just as the sports team board is utterly animated by the shape and printing on name tags, this scientist's certainty that the real world is physical always transcends his attention and behavior in service to the obstacles he knows are there. His imagination stops at the wall where content stops. Knowing seems to be a prize not worth winning.

A professor I know is a context addict. She dislikes content. It annoys her. If it is in the nature of a thing, rather than an idea, she recoils. She dislikes processes and procedures as well. She says, *Let others build track for the train to run on*. She loves vision, possibilities, reframing problems, commitment, and inquiry. When asked to pay attention to content, she finds others to do it. If pressed, she will do it herself, but without luster or the success she has when in a contextual conversation.

However, I also know a financial vice president whose life had been all about measurement and numbers. He started to see possibilities and was never the same. He became creative in the service of customers and employees, instead of assessing them all the time. While still a hard-driving, alpha male leader, he started to see his company in terms of its relationships and found a new way to get the job done more happily, and lost no experience of power.

If you change the domain in which you know something, a new world of imagining outside the box becomes possible.

EXPLANATION IS A BOX

Everybody is explaining all the time. Some of it makes sense as when you tell the doctor how you cut your hand. However, most explanation is a confounding waste of time and a barrier to imagination. This barrier to imagination is so challenging, I started *Explainers Anonymous,* a nonprofit organization dedicated to helping people addicted to explaining everything.

Our motto is: *The less you know,*
the longer the explanation.[9]

Dogs don't explain anything. Maybe that's why they seem so at peace. For us, explanation magically becomes the context for everything else. It seems innocent, except that most people I know

---

9   Brian Herbert and Kevin Anderson, the *Dune* series

have so many explanations that their mental box is full. There is no room to imagine. Some watch the Weather Channel and life is shaped by expectations of rain or not. Some won't travel to see their kids because they explain to themselves that they are too tired. Their explanation for not traveling keeps them from the life they could otherwise have.

In a diesel engine company I worked with, no one ever felt affirmed because sales targets were so high they never reached them. Despite positive results, they always disappointed bosses, financial analysts, and each other. They were depressed and had no joy at work because they were constantly explaining why they'd failed.

Explaining does not need to be a problem. Telling a story to entertain or teach is wonderful. It's when a person *has to* explain that the cycle of addiction begins. *Explainers Anonymous* was created in an attempt to help those who can't help explaining and have thereby lost their ability to imagine something else.

Sometimes, explanations are useful, so long as everyone understands it's an explanation, and only one out of many imagined possibilities. Sometimes they are important warnings, such as, *Look both ways before crossing the street because you might get hurt.*

But every day most of us wake up into a sea of explanations. There are TV channels with multitudes of explanations. There are religious explanations. There are Democratic and Republican explanations. Everybody has clay feet, but the explanations always make the speakers right and their adversaries wrong. I wish they would find something else to talk about. It all comes with an ulterior motive, which is to sell something or to get and maintain power. Always, it stops their ability to imagine a better world.

While built into many corporate and public governance structures in a sensible and limited context, explanation often breeds increased scrutiny and becomes the coin of the realm.

Investment companies are everywhere stimulating urges to fearfulness or greed, blaring out stock market reports of fast made riches or how to avoid quick losses from plunging markets. Meantime, while explanations about why things happened or didn't in the market are usually spoken with conviction, they are often wrong. Sometimes the exact same reason is actually given as to why things got better or worse.

It's the same with advertising and public relations; women talking about men and men talking about women, or new age religions holding hands in circles, desperately seeking salvation by other means — my list is endless. Mostly, you can't believe explanations from anyone who is selling something. They are only telling the good part. It's not evil; it's just marketing hype, aimed at justifying their point of view and business interest.

LINEAR THINKING IS A BOX

Many of the challenges facing organizations are not problems; they are paradoxes full of entangled and conflicting forces that must get managed to achieve any kind of resolution. Cultural injunctions are often embedded among these, such as a global soap company I worked with wanting its leaders to ... *be aggressive, but don't rock the boat.*

Most education (conventional and religious), most families, media pundits, advertising, and company cultures feed people right-wrong, either-or solutions, posit good guys versus bad guys, and stress the importance of answers. We usually get graded and promoted for the quality of our answers. We teach people to dislike confusion.

You don't find many people walking around, asking each other questions that don't have simple answers. *Who won the White Sox game?* is not a paradox. *What to do about the future of climate change?* gets closer and at least requires dialogue.

Most of the world's big challenges, and many of our personal ones as well, are not problems; they are paradoxes. A problem is a question raised for solution, for something to be done. It can be an unsettled question, or a difficulty in accepting or understanding, as in, *I have a problem with you saying that.* A problem can be fixed. I'm thirsty, so I drink, and the problem goes away.

A paradox is not the same as a problem.[10] A paradox is a set of conflicting forces, opposing vectors, drivers and stoppers, and questions without answers — and whichever way you go, you run into another wall.

---

10 David Bohm, *On Dialogue*, Routledge, 1996

An energy CEO recently told me, *I'm committed to my people — all of my people — keeping their jobs,* and *I have to take $150 million in costs out of this year's budget.* A results-driven, cause-and-effect thinking man or woman has a devil of a time with paradox. They keep insisting that they are dealing with a problem and go about trying to fix it. The difficulty is that paradoxes won't get fixed.

The best you can do with paradox is to dialogue with the people involved, in a search for shared meaning. Some solutions will emerge as you think together, but ultimately you live with it and learn to manage it, or find a way to create a bigger paradox, within which the first one seems to disappear.

Bohm proposes that thought itself is largely a collective phenomenon, even though it seems to us that we are each individually doing the thinking.[11] If so, then it is only through open-ended dialogue that shared meaning and unification can occur. Debate, opinion, and sharing information are not dialogue and rarely result in shared meaning.

A *paradox* seems contradictory or opposed to common sense, yet is perhaps true. It can be a self-contradictory statement, e.g., *My girlfriend is a wonderful woman, but I don't want to see her often.* It can be an inquiry filled with contradictory elements that do not easily resolve.

---

11   *Wholeness and the Implicate Order,* Routledge Classics, 1980

Bohm points out that *while a problem can be solved, a paradox cannot. And worse, the harder you try to solve a paradox, the worse it gets.*[12]

I believe that meaningful dialogue comes from grappling with paradoxes and finding some degree of shared meaning with others that might sometimes be the basis of action and other times not. Forcing solutions on paradoxes is ineffective, yet leaders try to do it all the time.

Getting comfortable with paradox is a necessary element in coming to think for oneself. Confusing problems with paradoxes helps keep the people in power in power, because you accept what they say or they control what you hear.

Next is a list of famous paradoxes. If you think them irrelevant, consider that paradox opens the mind and is a gateway to learning how to navigate from the future.

Hofstedder's Law: It always takes longer than you expect, even
       if you take into account Hofstedder's law.

Epimenides paradox: A Cretan says, "All Cretans are liars."

Exception paradox: If there is an exception to every rule, then
       every rule must have at least one exception, the excep-
       tion to this one being that it has no exception.

---

12   *On Dialogue*, op cit

Liar paradox: "This sentence is false." This is the canonical self-referential paradox. Also, "Is the answer to this question, 'No'?"

Petronius' paradox: Moderation in all things, including moderation.

Smale's paradox: A sphere can be turned inside out.

Schrödinger's Cat paradox: A quantum paradox — is the cat alive or dead before we look?

Quine's paradox: "...yields a falsehood when appended to its own quotation," yields a falsehood when appended to its own quotation.

Zeno's Dichotomy paradox: You will never reach point B from point A, as you must always get halfway there, and half of the next half, and half of that half, and so on.

Golden's paradox: A paradox comprised of the question, *What question has no answer?* Since all questions have answers, the answer to this particular question would be *This question.* While the question still contains an answer, the answer to the question states that it does not exist.

Abilene paradox: People make a decision based not on what they actually want to do, but on what they think other people want to do, with the result that everybody decides to do something that nobody really wants to do.

Paradox of Hedonism: When one pursues happiness itself, one is miserable; but, when one pursues something else, one achieves happiness.

The Irresistible Force paradox: What would happen if an unstoppable force hits an immovable object?

Omnipotence paradox: Can God make a rock too heavy to lift?

Consider that treating a paradox as if it were a problem stifles imagination and the possibility of a new future.

THE NAVIGATOR CODE

You have to believe it before you can see it.

A *navigator* has commitments, beliefs, and stories that help create gateways between people and groups, making radical breakthroughs and collective innovation possible.

COMMITMENT TO OTHERS' SUCCESS
IS THE PHILOSOPHER'S STONE

Middle Ages alchemists sought the "Philosopher's Stone," which could turn base metal into gold. In modern life, the base metal is everything that suppresses energy, cooperation, and willingness to reach beyond the predictable.

Most of the time, leaders and people in general become committed to others' success only so long as those others are doing what they want done. It's not that they are necessarily *against* each other, but they are just not being *for* one another. There are many reasons for this: natural reactions to hierarchy and squeezing into unnatural roles and functions, human nature and the fear of domination, having one's feelings hurt, etc.

Commitment to others' success is the singular basis of a navigator's *success.*

It is the platform from which a *navigator* inspires others with a sense of what's possible and helps them focus on what they are capable of, rather than just what they do. It is the Philosopher's Stone from which transformative solutions to problems of the earth and humanity become possible, i.e., cheap, widely available energy and propulsion; national security; health care; nutrition; community; family; poverty; sustainability; climate change; and governance.

In any situation, people are either "for" one another or they are not. This is absolute. When someone is asked if someone else is for them, the answer is always, *Yes, they are for me,* or *No, they are not for me.* You might say, *I can't tell,* which, as a practical matter, has the same effect as the other person not being for you.

This condition *is* the decisive framework of the relationship. It shapes what's possible and what happens. It either promotes energy, cooperation, and trust or suppresses them. Ultimately, it determines the quality of performance.

Business and technical processes are essentially conceptual in nature.
Commitment to others' success is not.
It's visceral. It's declarative. It's chemistry.
It doesn't follow predictable rules.

Gold — the possibility of learning, the free play of imagination — was missing in my kids' schooling. At ages seven and ten, they were not reading well, didn't particularly like books, and went to school mostly to play. By spring break there appeared to be more teacher neurosis than learning. Key staff had been fired and replaced, and the parental rumor mill was expanding exponentially, with even teachers and staff getting involved, including an assertion that as yet unreleased pre-post test results alarmingly indicated that the majority of the children had made little, if any, academic progress over the prior seven months.

The director, under multiple layers of personal and professional duress, had abandoned her espoused commitment to individual children's success, well-being, and self-esteem, replacing this with a newfound willingness (for herself and her staff) to humiliate them to make a point, particularly in the domains of orderliness and compliance. What had started with enormous promise was turning out terribly disappointing.

In the midst of myriad discussions about what was happening and what should be done, we received a phone request to come pick up our seven-year old, because he had disturbed a field trip. I arrived to find the director "dressing him down" publicly and informing him that his punishment would be denial of his participation in the year-end theatrical performance (a totally unrelated event, for which he had rehearsed very hard and was keenly anticipating). In turn, I accused her of not knowing how to manage him and lacking necessary creativity.

Arriving home with him, my wife and I addressed our son's pain and my fury with a thorough review of the turmoil we had been experiencing and observing in others over the past few weeks. We determined to begin homeschooling immediately. If the school was not going to be responsible for our kids' education and well-being, we would take it on ourselves. Given the circumstances, we felt confident we could do no worse.

In that moment, I saw that our minds were their future. Their ability to navigate from the future for themselves, to love and contribute in the world, was not going to come from schools playing out ineffective commitments on the blackboard of their lives. Suppression of their independent minds had become the order of the day, even in the shadow of brilliant education innovator, Maria Montessori.

What we really wanted for our kids was buried under the limitations and constraints of the system and the personalities involved. When school leaders' commitments to their agendas, procedures, and their own comforts became senior, along with narrow definitions of harmony and order, the children's individual needs and interests took second place.[13]

Whatever liberty had been in the boy's schooling had disappeared, leaving behind "order" masquerading as educational process. The process in our kids' school had become more committed to its internal consistencies than to our kids' ability to think, let alone empowering them to choose appropriate behavior for themselves.

---

13   (Note: As we have engaged in conversations about homeschooling over the intervening years, it seems a widely held view that children's individual needs and interests rarely get addressed at all in our school systems, unless they occur as "disturbances" to a picture of what "should be" – problems to be handled. *CS)*

As soon as we took responsibility for the quality of their education into our own hands, transformation happened. Either you have the system or the system has you.

WHO WILL LEAD?

Years ago, a very successful business friend observed that 10 percent of the people do everything. *Ten percent*, he insisted, *are cause in the matter of their own lives.* Ten percent create structures in which they and others operate. The other ninety percent eat at other people's tables and experience themselves under someone else's influence, even if they are bosses, parents, or have other formal authority.

The power to generate independently comes from navigating from the future. In any given moment, we and our children experience ourselves as either causing what is happening to us or living "at the effect" of it. It's a constant challenge to free ourselves from others' moods, demands, and preferences. If we go along most of the time, we become servants of others' systems, whether at work, school, or in the family.

When we stepped outside the box and into homeschooling, our boys became students, often achieving a free play in imagination and ability to think from a remarkable future. We entered a parallel universe in which commitment to each other's success, the act of being completely *for* each other's development and well-being, defined our path and gave us the ability to conceive a better world, a better family, and a future that didn't already exist.

The experience and lessons of homeschooling elaborated the possibility of learning to think more broadly from the future…and of a world that might not look like this one, but which called us to it nonetheless. In retrospect, there was a powerful, unspoken pledge from us to our boys:

- We are *for* you.
- We will not let what comes between us stay unresolved.
- We will make sure we are living into the same future at the highest level.
- We will not undermine you.
- We will not lie to you or withhold what you need to know to improve.
- We will be willing to have upsets happen between us.
- We will try to resolve differences and to speak out for the resolution of differences, privately and in public.
- We will not avoid public conversation about differences in order to maintain control.
- We will speak out for the value and validity of commitment to each other's success.

We demonstrated how absolute commitment to the quality of someone's education changes the future.

At first, it was a struggle as to who would prevail. To avoid schoolwork, they used every trick, half truth, and emotional plea that I had mastered in my own years in public school. Then, homeschooling became a miracle. The boys often slept late in the mornings, but then went to work with little cajoling. They focused mainly on subjects that interested them. Over time, after testing, if they proved weak in necessary skills, attention was focused and they improved rapidly.

Commitment to others' success is a kaleidoscope that the mind tries to freeze in time with images, pictures, and agreements. The experience keeps changing and, in any present moment, is never the same. My relationship to the earth I walk on, or the woman I love, or my favorite client, is never the same as it was. All that really stays the same is my commitment to them.

CONTEXT IS DECISIVE

The CEO of a large energy company recently asked me how he could possibly get his ten thousand employees into the same company boat. My suggestion was that we consider and grapple with the need for employees to follow their own destiny with the same conviction as we pursued shareholder wealth. He agreed.

Navigating from the future and respect for essence go together.

Over time it makes people crazy to make them do what they do not love. Focusing training on job requirements and organizational needs exclusively, instead of attending to what calls people as individuals, makes for a violent and uncooperative sensibility.

Like teaching our children to navigate from the future, what's called for is continual recognition that each of us has an essence, a destiny, a purpose, a core genius that evokes the best in us and in everyone around us.

Like many parents, as we wondered how to choose among the massive array of "elective" activities available, together with the kids we identified particular talents, skills, abilities they wanted to have in their lives, and then searched for places and ways for them to acquire those capabilities.

We heard, *If I could do anything, I think I might like to be a movie star,* and enrolled them into acting classes. Before long they auditioned and were given opportunities to perform in film and TV productions. They opted for a stage performance summer program instead of a sports-oriented camp. Within only a few months, one declared a continuing serious interest in acting, while the other shifted focus to directing and the technical aspects of stage and film production, with distinctions and perspectives on the subject that were quite remarkable.

Becoming a great photographer and maybe working for National Geographic took one into photography classes. Watching the Sydney Olympics led the other to a diving class at the Y. *Learning a lifetime sport* led one to tennis lessons and tryouts for a school team. *Liking to make experiments* led to a weekly class at the local science museum. Enjoying the game of chess led both to an after-school club and community league play.

In each of these cases, the boys saw their training classes as necessary steps to an end result *they* wanted to achieve. They pursued studies in scuba, Tae Kwon Do, ballroom dancing, archery, and medieval weaponry. Experiences in following their bliss moved them in different directions and created visions of possible futures and pursuits that were not previously available, to them or to us.

Adjacent possibilities, adjacent futures, emerged at the speed of light, and there was not enough time in the days and weeks to include all the pursuits they found appealing. Enthusiasm and excitement were noticeable more days than not, and their learning was enormous.

It is the same in companies, when the commitment is to make the place work for everyone, with respect and responsibility.

COMBINE NOBLE PURPOSE AND PRAGMATIC PURPOSE

The idea of combining entrepreneurial business success with noble purpose is countercultural. When I suggested it to one of my colleagues, he got angry and wanted no part of it. *It's nonsense,* he said. *The purpose of business is business, and trying to do something else with it will be unsuccessful and damaging.*

A former client is an alpha male and successful, and anything that sounds soft scares him. He told me directly, *I don't want you using words like* noble purpose *around here.* I thought he was going to say it was evil.

Noble purpose is whatever someone says is an important contribution in service of others. My idea of a noble purpose may not be the same as yours. We find that these social concerns are unique to individual CEOs, and have ranged from the future of their state or community to energy independence, space, security, health and nutrition, family, poverty, sustainability, climate change, governance, and other such issues.

Nobody seems to have gotten this quite right. In 1953, former General Motors president Charles Wilson famously said, *What's good for our country is good for General Motors, and vice versa.* (Wilson later became Secretary of Defense for the United States.) Communism, starting out with grand visions of social responsibility, observably deteriorated into authoritarian dictatorships, weak economies, and few civil liberties.

Capitalism, in its pure form, leaves social responsibility in the hands of charities, religions, and government. It's a much more productive system that raises the standard of living for many people, but only so long as its elites are kept from turning the system to their own advantage at any social cost.

Hylan Lyon, science advisor to three US presidents, contributed in our discussions:

Noble Purpose is not an elevated sense of social consciousness. It is a pragmatic admission of what's required to successfully pursue large markets over time and geography that encompass cultural differences. It is the recognition that when you explain your value proposition, much of its worth is embedded in your ability to recognize and respond appropriately to local value systems. The common values that hold across these diversities always relate to what all of the customers, in the whole, deeply care about, and how your product enables them to see the linkage.

There are increasing numbers of companies with examples of performance aspirations beyond normal. They want to do something for the world with values-based, realizable propositions within their existing businesses, as well as through additions, partnerships, and niche markets that fit with what they already do. Many are recognized with awards and "ratings" produced by magazines and industry associations.

In June 2008, *Ethisphere Magazine* assessed and published a list of the one hundred "Most Ethical" companies in the world, which included Google, Honeywell International, Timberland, BMW, Honda, Oracle, American Express, General Mills, Marriott Hotels, Marks and Spencer, and UPS. The publishers noted that "The World's Most Ethical Companies are the ones that go above and beyond legal minimums, [and] bring about innovative new ideas to expand the public well being…"

Is it an impossible dream for business to be responsible for society? If taken seriously, would most do a more efficient job than governments? We will never find out without blocking inattention to noble purpose.

Unthinkably bold goals interrupt memories of
past successes and failures,
fears, and mind-driven limitations.

Whether it is reaching for one hundred million dollars' profit, having a great relationship, or getting support for a world-altering energy technology, unpredictable, ambitious goals and quantum leaps *are* the way to keep life exciting, to keep from getting bored, and to make unimaginable progress. The security and predictability that come from incremental goals are comforting and boring. Passion creates confidence.

We sell our souls at the altar of the incremental.

☯

A Shaolin Monk Walks Through Walls
David Carradine, *Kung Fu*

The box is mostly in your mind.

Of course, this is not the box that tells you if you jump off the roof you will die. There are real boxes out there. But *most* are products of our thinking. You can get outside of the boxes in your mind and imagine something brilliant, or at least different from what you already think.

Quotes and one-liners have been my bread and butter for forty years. One-liners metaphorically point to answers that won't come from simple sentences or less simple paragraphs. "Getting out of the box" and "walking through walls" are great metaphors. There is really no box there, though it sure seems like there is. Nobody *makes* you be careful or to play small. No one *makes* you work where you work. Still, they are parts of your box, and as real as if there were a physical box there surrounding you.

Vitality, health, and self-expression come from thinking you have an inspired future. Deadness comes from being stuck. Sure there are jobs where you might get fired if you speak out. But how will you ever know?

Shaolin monks walk through walls because they know that, usually, the wall is not really there.

FROM IMPOSSIBILITY ANYTHING FOLLOWS

Block the impossible. Noticing what is impossible and asking what you would have to do to make it possible blocks the suppressive experience of impossibility and frees imagination to think from the future. The act of taking responsibility for yourself as the creator of possibility puts the mind to work on the right problem, which is making yourself, whether a person or group, responsible for being the cause of possibility. The block goes away.

Thinking something is impossible blocks imagination. People only think about what they see as possible. Often, what's impossible for them never gets conscious. It's like being inside a house and not knowing there is an outside.

For a plant manager I know, there is no possibility of vision. There is only work. To one financial vice president I know, there is only the world of making money. He can't imagine a world in which not making money could exist. It's a flat earth, and he thinks he could fall off.

Facing up to a personal truth of "no possibility" *and* taking responsibility for what you would have to do to create it are remarkably and surprisingly effective. One woman would never consider buying an expensive house until she faced that it was not possible *and* what she would have to do to make it possible. She saw that she would have to promise to earn a specific amount of money, and at the same time mean it. Suddenly, in seeing that she could mean it, it became possible.

One young manager *could not* set an ambitious, unreasonable goal. When asked what he could do to make such a goal possible, he said that to create the possibility he would have to be willing to live with an unthinkable fear for the few moments it would take to think of the goal. He chose to do that, and all of a sudden it was possible!

A consumer goods manufacturing team identified the impossibility of increasing machine efficiencies. When asked what they would have to do to make it possible, they said that they would have to break the company's manual regulations. Suddenly, the possibility was there, and they doubled machine efficiencies in a matter of weeks.

BEWARE OF SIMULATIONS OF GOD

In the 1970s, scientist and author John Lilly wrote that human behavior is entirely *Simulations of God*[14]. In other words, it's all religion and belief, up and down the line, and everyone has some-

---

14   *Simulations of God: The Science of Belief,* mass market paperback, 1976

thing they consider to be God. For some, it's a religious figure. For others, it's money, power, glory, or control. For some, if you look closely, it is to feel that they are special — to be a mother, a father, an athlete. Whomever or whatever you consider to be your higher power, that's the cornerstone and guiding principle, the prime directive, of your life.

For some, Planet Earth or even the future of humans in space is the field of play. For many others, the field upon which life is played is closer to the size of a postage stamp. Postage stamp lives can be seen in youth gangs defending their blocks as the ground of the known universe; in opinionated talk show hosts bashing anybody and anything outside the confines of their ideology; in religious leaders implicitly declaring that they are closer to God than those who believe differently or, God forbid, those who don't believe at all.

In teaching our children to navigate from the future, we wanted to stay as far away from postage stamp realities as we could. It seemed to us that romance, looking to the stars, and taking Planet Earth and all its people as the frame for our picture would help our quest for independent thinking. We wanted them to be able to think from the whole of things, or from as much of the whole as we ourselves could reach.

Teaching others to think beyond what they already know is both a solitary and a collective act. Educated men and women have knowledge of books and information generated from outside their own simulations of God. To keep seeking such sources in the face of our own preferences as to what is true, just, or sacred is a necessary aspect of the process. Pushing beyond what we already knew proved to be a postage stamp without limits, often not easy to lick and stick onto locally approved envelopes.

ㆍ❦ㆍ

It's not what you do. It's what you are capable of.
Kirsten Anderson, coach
(Orlando Area Rowing Society)

Block what you *can* do. On the starting line for our son's rowing club, I was holding the back of a women's "Varsity Four" boat in place for the start of the race. The wind blew, and the water was rough. They knew what they were doing and kept the boat pointed in the right direction. Just before the race started, the small coxswain, a girl directing from the stern, said in a strong voice, *Remember, girls, it's not what you do. It's what you are capable of.*

They took off with force and conviction. I was thunderstruck with the power of her words and what they had learned from their coach. In that moment, I realized I'd been living my life in great part merely from what I could do and not from what I'm capable of, and that this was true at work, at home, and in contributing to the world. I entered a parallel universe of adjacent possibilities, in which capability, not normalcy, ruled the day. By speaking as she did, the coxswain had blocked what I had been doing to undermine my imagination and what I am capable of.

I rushed home and wrote down everything that I am capable of and knew it would happen. In the moment of blocking one approach, a new one occurred.

Transformation is not the result of a process. It's an *all of a sudden* phenomenon, a quantum leap phenomenon — from what I already did to what I am capable of.

You can *promise what you can't predict.*
Werner Erhard

It *is* possible to promise something that can't be predicted. Obvious, but uncommon. Most people don't do it, and most won't do it when given the opportunity. Most promise what they can predict and live, therefore, in an endless cycle of doing what they already know how to do, accomplishing what they already accomplish.

Maybe it's fear of failure, or fear of success, or fear of being called to be something more than we think we are. Most won't do it, and hardly anyone does it regularly. Still, when you look at many of the world's great accomplishments, promising what couldn't be predicted is just what's happened.

Consider the winning of World War II — unconditional surrender was the goal, and all the resources were incessantly devoted to that end. Ever since then, this kind of victory has not been promised.

There are always good reasons for not promising, and no other war has been "won." Only if the commitment is strong enough will you make such promises, even up against strong reason and arguments against it.

I know that when I promise what I can't predict, something uncharacteristic kicks in — some attention to getting real, some urgency, some level of action and being real that is never available from planning or making promises for what I already know I can do.

Until one is committed, there is hesitancy,
the chance to draw back, always ineffectiveness.
Concerning all acts of initiative, there is one elementary truth,
the ignorance of which kills countless ideas
and splendid plans:

The moment one definitely commits oneself,
then Providence moves too.

All sorts of things occur to help one that would never otherwise
have occurred. A whole stream of events issues from the decision,
raising in one's favor all manner of unforeseen incidents and
meetings and material assistance, which no man could have
dreamed would have come his way.[15]

---

15   Scottish mountaineer William Hutchinson Murray

Whatever you can do, or dream you can, begin it.
Boldness has genius, power and magic in it.
Begin it now.[16]

⚭

Force Causes Resistance.

Sir Isaac Newton

Anything you resist persists. The more you resist something, the more it resists you back. In Star Trek episodes, the Borg, a deadly interplanetary force, would leave people alone so long as no one got in its way. If they stood in its path, they were devastated. The more I resist you, the more you will resist me. It's a formula for success, or a formula for failure.

Mike McMaster, an experienced management consultant and friend, once noted that the surest way to suppress people's creativity is to put them in a hierarchy. Immediately the rules of a top-dog, under-dog game begin. Compliance with real or imagined hierarchical force suppresses mood and creates resignation. Most people play the game, going along with the rules and, by degrees, losing their spontaneity.

These reactionary consequences of the use of force are difficult to separate from the merits of any situation. You may be

---

16   German writer Johann Wolfgang von Goethe

right, but your forcefulness can prevent anyone from listening to you. With our sons, we used stories from the American Civil War as examples of men and women on both sides who would not just go along. We pointed to Kirk Douglas' *Spartacus*, the film where he led a slave rebellion against Rome, and to various anti-establishment political candidates and movements, to demonstrate how hierarchical force has produced equal and opposite effects.

Of course, it's possible to be in a hierarchical company, family, or school *and* be imaginative. It calls for vigilance. Carlos Castaneda suggested that *stalking knowledge is like going to war, and calls for special attention.*[17] I wanted our boys to be able to recognize when they are simply in a hierarchy and how to remain free by not resisting, but by thinking from the future and making their own choices.

There is no secret ingredient. There is only you.

Kung Fu Panda

What is a *possibility creator*? FedEx did not exist, and then it did. The same with Microsoft, and with the idea of human rights — one day, they were not there, nowhere to be found, and then they were! In the millisecond between the idea and the image, *there* was possibility. The possibility of imagining something *always* precedes it.

Most people I've known have not been able to create the possibility of anything they consider impossible. I know a hotel company vice president who cannot conceive the possibility of anything working that is not ordered and tidy. A client who's a manufacturing executive cannot imagine the possibility of a company in which he simply does what others ask. A friend who's an oil and gas engineer cannot see the possibility of a world in which his is not the only and supreme God. The leader of a global food business can only imagine a company in which attention to processes reigns supreme.

At our best, we are *possibility creators*. At our worst, we are instead, *no possibility* creators. This has been affirmed since 1854, when Henry David Thoreau said, *the mass of men lead lives of quiet desperation.*[17] What we call "resignation" is confirmed desperation. Resignation comes from *no possibility.*"

Possibility comes only *from you.*

Michael Reid, a brilliant thinker and teacher, noted that a new possibility is the same as a new context or a new framework from which to think, live, and work. There is no "real" possibility in the world. Possibility has no physical existence. It is either a linguistic event or some inexplicable thing that happens when people's creative energies take over.

But most people didn't create their companies or their jobs. Most people born into a worker culture never create the possibility of becoming a member of some elite, and vice versa. Most religious

---

17   *Walden; or, Life in the Woods,* Ticknor and Fields (Original Publisher), Boston, 1854

people believe in the God they found in their childhood homes. This is not necessarily bad; it just rarely changes.

When change does happen, it's because the person has somehow declared, if not in words then in deed, that he or she is a *possibility creator*, and then proven it. My cousin Warren, from the declaration that he would never be cold again, amassed a billion-dollar fortune. He determined that he would eat at his own table, created the possibility, and did it.

DON'T BE A NOODLE IN SOMEONE ELSE'S SOUP

Being a noodle in another's soup makes a child, or an executive, or anyone, a candidate for a life of energy loss and quiet resignation. That this resignation has become a widespread malady is often apparent on people's faces — in the street, in corporate corridors, even between estranged couples sitting together in restaurants with nothing to say.

There seems to be an endless variety of noodle possibilities: women's soup, men's soup, macho soup, materialism soup, religious soup, political soup, culture soup, and correct behavior soup. Every moment is filled with offers, answers, warnings, protections, distractions, and entertainments. Implicit, always, is a message about who makes the rules, who is the cook, and whose bowl the soup comes in.

While no one likes to be dominated, few master this noodle phenomenon, which is to stay out, or at least be able to move in and out of other people's soup at will.

In teaching our sons to think for themselves, we pointed out the seductive magnetism of commercials, marketing offers, and promises of emotional or financial salvation. However intelligent-seeming, any promise that their lives will be better *because of x* includes a dark side that comes with the invitation to jump into the speaker's soup bowl.

Like Pinocchio, we can all be too easily seduced into an "amusement park" only to discover ourselves alone in a prison of unimagined horrors and isolation from our own truth.

Take the path less traveled.

Robert Frost[18]

John Kennedy is attributed with saying that *if you see something that is very well organized, you can be sure that not much is really going on.*

"Herd" behavior is everywhere. Sitting in the Charlottesville airport — small, cute, reminding me of the airport in the movie *Casablanca* — I waited. Trying unsuccessfully to meditate, I noticed that there were forty people sitting, side by side, next to the gate. I had moved to another gate area, which was empty. The rest of the airport was empty.

---

18 "The Road Not Taken," *Mountain Interval,* 1916

Why did they all sit together, when there is all this room? People always bunch up, sit side by side, and stare at the backs of each other's heads. *Schools and organizations really are doing their jobs,* I thought. These people have been trained to sit together quietly inside a box they don't see. They had to be operating inside a set of rules about sitting quietly in rows, near an authority, a teacher, next to one another, etc. I wouldn't have been surprised if they had all folded their hands in their laps, as well.

Some years ago at a political rally on The Mall in Washington, DC, I heard a speaker say, *There are two choices in life – to either be a gangster or an outlaw. The gangsters rip off the public and the outlaws rip off the gangsters.* In the movies, my heart goes out to the outlaws and bridles at the gangsters — people taking advantage of the public.

Navigators are mavericks — independent individuals who don't reflexively go along with any group or party. Joseph Campbell said that *it is impossible to get away from the system. We are all in it. But,* he said, *you do not have to become an agent of the system.*[19] A system is a machine, and when you become its agent, you become a machine and lose your humanity. To not become an agent of any system is to take the path less traveled.

---

19   in an interview with Bill Moyers on PBS, *The Power of Myth,* based on Campbell's book of the same name, 1988

We shall not cease from exploration
And the end of all our exploring
Will be to arrive where we started
And know the place for the first time.

.., a condition of complete simplicity
(Costing not less than everything)
And all shall be well and
All manner of thing shall be well
When the tongues of flames are in-folded
Into the crowned knot of fire
And the fire and the rose are one.

T.S. Eliot, *Four Quartets*

✎

BEGINNER'S MIND

Much of the time, people are walking concepts. If you are not thinking, you are more open to possibilities. Buddhism makes a convincing case for meditation to empty the mind. Yoga works, as do sports and walks on the beach.

Eckhart Tolle says, *There is a vast realm of intelligence — everything of true value — love, art, nature, outside the mind.* [20] He calls it

---

20   *The Power of Now*, New World Library, 2004

being. It's the same as your experience of your own presence. When you sense your own presence, you are not thinking; you are just *there*…with the sky or a child you love.

Navigating from the future begins with the clarity that comes from such presence. Sustainable transformation in business is hard to find. It calls for leaders, groups, and families being determined *not* by the past but by practicing the power of such presence. As Peter Sellers portrayed in his final movie, it calls for *Being There.*

A fine technique is to practice *Beginner's Mind.*

Meeting an interesting European couple for the second time, I was eager for the conversation. When we'd first met, we sparked with ideas about politics, child rearing, what kind of country we wanted to live in, and just about everything else. I was looking forward to the same quality of conversation.

As I began to share my excitement about what I was working on, I felt surprised and deflated as the wife was immediate with comments that showed she already knew everything I was talking about. I wondered if we'd had too much to drink at our first meeting and whether she had been doing this then as well. She was an expert in anything I had to say. In one instance, I said only half a sentence on purpose, and she finished it, with something far removed from what I would have said! I'd met an expert on the road and wished she wasn't there. I felt dishonored and any experience of possibility disappeared.

- *Beginner's Mind* requires approaching a situation with few preconceptions or questions. It requires us to listen and appreciate.
- *Beginner's Mind* induces presence and relationship, and lets others know that we respect them.
- *Beginner's Mind* honors whoever you are with and allows for navigating from the future.
- *Beginner's Mind* allows imagination to find a home.

It helps to ask questions to which you don't know the answer. Answers, and techniques that work in some circumstances, don't work all the time. They always intersect with mood and circumstance, Karma and fate.

What makes a difference is not an answer. Lists of solutions don't help. Even help doesn't help. What makes a difference is *imagining from the future to the present.*

❦

Discovery is exciting, and implementation is boring, unless you maintain the spirit of the voyage. What makes a difference is to implement and, at the same time, keep inquiring. The organizational world thrives on implementation and generally loses the passion of invention that keeps vitality alive.

Tony Robbins says, *The mind is a problem solving machine and answers only the questions you ask of it. When you keep asking the same questions, you will mostly get the same answers because the mind only looks at its own memories for data.* [21]

Quantum physics suggests that, at its core, the world consists of *possibilities that don't exist until a question is asked.*

If you want to think from the future and put your imagination to work, you have to ask questions to which you don't already have the answer. Then, the chances of real thinking go up.

Sticking with questions to which you already know the answer, or the approximate answer, keeps you in a past-based vicious circle. Martin Heidegger taught us that *thinking only happens when a topic is worthy of thought.* [22] The needed training and practice is in blocking questions to which you already know the answer.

THE BRAIN CAN BE REWIRED

Norman Doidge [23] makes the case for plasticity in the brain and demonstrates that neuronal activity, which is now measurable, can be increased and expanded through training and practice in the same ways that are producing medical marvels with autism, blindness, neurological disorders, and strokes.

Imagine that the same plasticity is there for developing our ability to think from the future. *Blocking* is where it begins. If you don't block

---

21   *Personal Power: A 30-Day Program,* audio cassettes, 1993
22   *Basic Writings,* Routledge, 1993
23   *The Brain That Changes Itself,* op cit

what's already there, not much that's new can show up. *How can I imagine something new if I can't replace what's already there? How can I look for something different if there is no possibility of something different?*

You can't give the mind a new rule where there is already a rule. The first step is to make room for something new. You can't fill a cup that's full. The first discipline is to empty the cup.

Blocking happens when you do the opposite of what you normally do. It happens when you find a way to suppress or negate what you usually do. *Blocking* can happen when you enlist an outside source to do it for you, with your permission.

In Doidge's research he found that people who were kept in a completely dark room for extended periods of time developed sensitive hearing ability, akin to that of a blind person. He found scientific research showing that stroke victims who were not allowed to use their one good arm for long training periods developed use of their paralyzed arm. He found that people who were trained to imagine lifting weights with their arms developed 22 percent muscle mass, compared to test groups who gained 30 percent muscle mass by actually lifting the weights.

Prevailing science has said that the brain was not plastic — that if an area of the brain devoted to a particular function was damaged, no correction was possible. Now, with the ability to scan neurons in the brain with great accuracy, it is being proven that, with a willing participant, the brain *can* be rewired, through blocking other adaptations and long training periods.

This has important implications for education, culture change in companies, personal or family dysfunction, and other areas where people repetitively behave in ineffective ways, feel trapped within their own mechanisms, and want to do otherwise.

According to Doidge's research, the longer the *blocking* occurs and the longer the subsequent training period, the longer lasting are the effects. At a point, the effects appear to either become permanent or satisfying.

PAY ATTENTION TO THE REAL WORLD

There are two worlds always occurring at the same time. One is physical and material. The other is the invisible world of relationship and human energy. Both are real. Both have impact. Either is ignored at one's own peril.

It is easier to see this when you are in the presence of something that can't be explained — the sea, fire, trees, flowers. *Who can explain a flower? Are we natural beings living in an unnatural world?*

Sitting on a beach watching the waves, or watching Taos Indians do the Deer Dance...none of this is scientific, unless you are a chemist or anthropologist, analyzing the mystery away.

In the modern world of productivity, consumption, and money, that which can be measured has become sacred. If it can be measured it is considered real. If it can't be measured, it is called unreal and sensed as a scary threat to productivity.

Measurement kills transformation. The more a relationship is measured, the less emotional connection there is. I prefer to live in a world full of radiance and emotional presence — not easy to do with the ever-present computer, phone, TV, and everybody selling something.

It is easy to pay attention to the "unreal" world of relationships, energy, and people's spirits for the sake of imagining and navigating from the future. Yet, given the domination of the "real" world, it takes a lot of intention.

ೞ

The Real World

I do not live in the real world,
But in a world fitted to the mind of man.

Condensed and busy
Congested and productive
Dominating and avoiding
Linear and squared

Economic and hierarchical
Technological and organized
Justified and sold
Parceled and bankable
Verbal unreal

I do not live in the real world,
except today.

In the vast emptiness of Creation,
awesome Creator and Creation are one.

In mist and sea,
in endless horizon,
beyond and before words,
I am living in the real world.

Charles E. Smith
(notes from Bangor, North Wales)

BLOCK PRIOR ATTEMPTS AT SOLUTION

I wanted to be a Lion Tamer, but was afraid,
so I tried to work it out as an accountant.
(derived from an Ernst and Young Sweden video)

Already knowing something is a block to imagination. If you take any problem that won't resolve and notice all prior attempts at solution, you will see that they have some things in common.[24]

Common to all prior attempts at revitalizing the US car industries is the repeated refusal to make small, fuel efficient cars, and ongoing assumptions about the size and loyalty of the American market.

Common to a consultant friend's financial problems is that he won't abide any experience of domination by a client, won't work for anyone he thinks is a jerk, and is convinced that they owe him an ongoing living once he's done a great initial job.

If you examine any persistent problem or situation of your own, you will see that all of your prior attempts at solution have some things in common. Whatever is common to all prior attempts at solution are the core reasons why our problems persist. These commonalities are the unseen context, the limiting boundary conditions that keep the past repeating itself.

Unless you can move against whatever is common and essentially block the doing of it, the past will repeat itself.

This is especially difficult since we successfully survived through these methods in past attempts. Subsequently, even when they fail,

---

24   *Pragmatics of Human Communication*, Paul Watzlawick, Janet Helmick Beavin, and Don D. Jackson, MD, WW Norton, 1967

we are afraid to let them go. New thinking, however, will come from blocking it.

ALWAYS SEEK SHARED COMMITMENT
BEFORE AGREEMENT

Agreement calls for a meeting of minds and may be fact-based or experience-based. *Alignment* is what people mean by "being in the same boat" or being "in it" together, or "headed in the same direction." Alignment produces common cause and "common sense." It is the process by which the boundary conditions for rational thought are set. Without alignment, there is no "higher purpose" reference point within which to resolve inevitable problems.

Reason and rationality cannot set their own boundaries. Rather, they follow rules of logic, within pre-established boundary conditions set by commitments already in place. Shared commitment is *prerequisite* to seeing what is actually missing and needed for moving forward. This logic is counterintuitive and flies in the face of most people's education, training, and opinion.

Hylan Lyon points out that alignment of thought, at the moment of commitment to a program, *preordains* the success or failure of the program, more than any physical technology or engineering challenge. That moment is more deterministic of success than nearly any challenge or seeming impossibility contained within the program.

Agreement *is* vital for creating an effective process. What's less obvious is that agreement does not assure that anything will actually happen. Commitment, not agreement, is the basis of action. There are countless good ideas, broadly agreed upon, about which technologies and public-private partnerships would undoubtedly work that never get acted upon. No matter how heartfelt or sincere, a good idea is not necessarily *committed.*

We all have the experience of participating in seemingly endless discussions that lead nowhere, because of the assumption that if something is a good idea it will be acted upon. It's just not true. Sincerity and logic do not get anything to happen. Commitment does. It is the failure to recognize that most conversations are not commitment-based that keeps lots of bright people spinning their wheels, ultimately becoming resigned to the notion that no one cares enough to act.

Unfortunately, we live in an agreement-based world, filled with agreement-based organizations. Almost everyone thinks that people need to agree in order to move forward. Consequently, countless fruitless hours are spent trying to change each other's minds, which is at best difficult and often impossible.

As we repeatedly fail to achieve agreement, we become more and more desensitized to the typical backup methods most commonly employed — command and control, maneuvering behind the scenes, conning, outwitting, and threatening, whether in subtle or direct ways. Since force causes resistance, things usually get worse.

In the absence of alternatives, this process endlessly repeats itself and we are caught in a continuous loop, futilely anticipating a different result.

STOP WISHING FOR THE WORLD YOU WANT

Most of the people I know avoid core truths like the plague. My friend tells enough of the truth about his wife to keep the marriage stable. A former client's employees tell the truth about him in private but never in public. The *king had no clothes,* and it took an innocent child to point it out. The Bible says that *the truth will set you free.* The core truth *will* set you free, but often it will first upset you.

Every time I've seen a core truth, the awful truth, the truth about what's *really* happening at the level of people's actual experience, there's been a short period of despair, *and then* a new possibility for improvement or completion. But fears abound — *I will look bad. I'm afraid. It won't help.* The resistance to telling the truth about one's own experience is endless.

Imagine there are two doors. One says *The Core Truth* and the other says *Lecture about the Core Truth.* There is no one in line for the truth, but a long line of people waiting to hear the lecture.

Not telling the core truth blocks imagination and navigating from the future. Not telling the core truth is like driving a car without your hands on the steering wheel.

Telling the core truth doesn't mean you have to be mean or cruel. But given the divorce rate, the waste in too many organizations, our infrastructure problems, and the pressures of an increasingly globalizing world, not telling our core truths and not acting on them is increasingly stupid.

For example, in a *New York Times* editorial (December 14, 2008), Tom Friedman asked:

What is the core truth about Detroit? Auto executives will tell you that it's the credit crisis, health care, retirement costs and unions. Sure, those are real. But the core truth is that, for way too long Detroit's made too many cars that too many people did not want to buy.

ଔ

Train yourself not to fear losing what you care for.
Yoda, *Star Wars*

Block codependence.

Codependence is a box that suppresses imagination. Codependence is when you feel compelled to have (or to induce) others' agreement, acceptance, or support before acting. Codependence in human affairs is like gravity in nature. It's everywhere and nearly impossible to escape. Even when you resist your own or others' codependence, it often seems to make matters worse.

For example:

- *What do you want, honey?*
  I don't know. What do you want?
- *What's good for business is good for America.*
- *Be careful; what does the boss really think?*
- *Without this job, this religion, this marriage,*
  this political party.., I would not exist.

Codependence is a disease, with guilt as a brother and shame as a sister. Breaking the rules *and* honoring the rules of codependence both drain energy. It is zombie training, and one size fits all.

Having to go along and having to not go along produce the same result. We first learn to be codependent with our parents, and eventually most of us want to stay away from them most of the time, even though we love them.

Codependence squeezes the life out of projects. No one ever wrote a poem or a love song about a corporation or a government agency. Who would love that which has such power, even when we've granted that power ourselves?

Codependence requires us to get someone else's agreement or compliance for our own attitudes and behavior. It is a box that slows evolution to a crawl.

In Every Moment there is an Entire Universe.

Star Trek: Insurrection

Block your black hole.

A black hole is a region of space in which the gravitational field is so powerful that nothing, not even electromagnetic radiation (e.g., visible light), can escape its pull after having fallen past its event horizon. The term derives from the fact that the absorption of visible light renders the hole's interior invisible, and indistinguishable from the black space around it.

Every person, every group, every company has a "show stopper" that is the equivalent of a black hole in human terms. It keeps people playing a small game, living and acting as if the rest of the world is like whatever is going on in their own minds.

Psychologist Eric Berne referred[25] to this phenomenon as a *racket,* a way of being, taking action, and achieving results that, while successful initially, has the eventual downside of suppressing your own and others' performance, vitality, and willingness to risk.

Many people become powerful through devotion to their racket. Napoleon, Hitler, Stalin, Mao Tse Tung, and countless alpha personalities have risen to the top by seeking to reform the world in their own image. For most of us, our black hole-like rackets are less dramatic, but pervasive, nevertheless.

---

25   *Games People Play: The Basic Handbook of Transactional Analysis,* Random House, 1996

Below are a few rackets I have observed in people I've worked with closely:

- A corporate vice president: *I can't let anyone be close to me.*
- A CEO: *I have to be reasonable.*
- A consultant: *I have to be smart and tough.*
- A scientist: *Why me? Why do I have to be the one?*
- An engineer: *That won't work because...*
- A lawyer: *I won't agree with anyone, ever.*
- A programmer: *Whatever you offer, I'll slip and slide.*
- A musician: *I don't talk to jerks.*
- A retail sales manager: *I am always afraid.*
- A plant manager: *I won't lose.*
- A managing director: *I have to seem nice.*
- An administrative assistant: *Whatever you say, I will be kind and arrogant.*
- A saleswoman: *I didn't do it... it's not my fault.*
- A managing partner: *If I don't look good, I will die.*

For most people, rackets are absolute. They are a universe unto themselves. Rackets are global. All individuals, as well as companies, nations, religions, tribes, and cultures, have a racket. Most leaders and people around the world would rather die than give up their personal or institutional rackets.

The bottom line, however, is that our rackets prevent cooperation by denying the reality of others' experience. When it comes to national and global security or protecting the planet from our own self-interest, our rackets will kill us all.

The more power and influence people have, the greater the suppressive effect of their rackets on cooperation and the truth about what's limiting greater success. There may be an entire universe in every moment, but the racket keeps each of us from finding out. It keeps us playing a smaller game than we otherwise would.

There are hundreds, maybe thousands, of rackets. But they are all flavors of the same ice cream. Some people's default reaction is to always say to themselves, *Why me?* and then withdraw. Others slip and slide, and never commit. Some stay under the radar and don't make waves. Still others are smart and aggressive, and squelch relationships, even those they need to succeed.

The function of a racket is to avoid the
domination of others, along with a fear of
independent thought and an uncertain future.

When people become acutely conscious of their pervasive, automatic responses — their auto pilot — they are usually better able to pay attention in areas where they typically don't, and subsequently, to see what is needed that was not evident to them beforehand. This objectivity is only available when one can recognize and set aside, if only for a moment, one's default reaction.

Block that which does not attract.
Create a Context that Resonates.

John Caswell
(Group Partners, Ltd)

There's a way of using language that creates the possibility of something new happening and that explains almost everything that already is happening. Call it *context* or *distinction*. It is like balance on a bicycle. With it you can ride the bike; without it you can't. You can't see it, can't even define it, but it's clearly there somehow, and shaping everything else that's going on when you're on a bicycle.

Color is not the color red, or the color blue, or the color green. *Color* is just like *balance* on the bicycle; it makes all the different colors possible. But without the context or the distinction of color you couldn't possibly get red or green. One day there was no human rights on the planet and the next day there was. What was it? Where did it come from?

It seems to me that much…most…maybe everything that's of true value — love, beauty, art, freedom, great relationship — is a *context* or *distinction*. They give the possibility of any number of forms. I am no longer just living on Planet Earth! All of a sudden, here is the ability see into the heart of what is *giving* the present reality — what is giving a good relationship, what is generating a successful team or a dysfunctional team, what is allowing for friendship or disallowing the same.

Context *is* what lets you see what is not there — what is missing, what is shaping what happens. I started to see the frame of the picture — that which was attracting the present reality, whether it was a conversation or a successful effort — whatever was *attracting it into existence.* Nothing seemed to actually happen or occur or manifest, unless it was attracted into existence by one of these distinctions or contexts.

With this insight, I began to have the same impact with 150-person groups that I'd had before with only five or six people at a time. I stopped paying so much attention to what people said, and listened instead for what they were committed to. I started listening for what they were *not* saying. Immediately I realized that what they were not saying was the underlying cause for what was happening.

> *Being able to see what is underneath,*
> *to see what is steering the ship in any system,*
> *is what gives the ability to win before you engage.*

Most everyone I know responds to what they see in front of them — their husbands, their wives, people they work for, people they work with, people who work for them. What's going on in front of them is what's real for them. The performance they see is what's real. The money they see is what's real. What's physically there is what's real.

What I came to see is that the context in the background, like balance on a bicycle, *is* what was giving that reality. If I could see through to that context, even name it, I would get access to power and the ability to influence, in a much broader way, and be more effective.

This is often a hard sell. Everybody reacts to what they think is real. What I'm saying is real isn't what they see. But it is that which attracts, and by definition, that which repels, that is steering the ship.

IMAGINE THE "OVERVIEW EFFECT"

The Overview Effect is the shift in identity recognized by Frank White in his book of the same name[26], as the experience shared by many astronauts as they look at Earth and the universe from space. White's riveting account of personal transformation at the level of perspective and concern for the entire planet creates the possibility of an Overview Effect as an element in formulating policy and alignment of thought among leaders.

These astronauts realized that arbitrary distinctions of political and economic boundaries are invisible, and better solutions to many issues would come from reconsidering world problems from that point of view.

White shares this experience, described by astronaut Rusty Schweickart at the Lindisfarne Conferences in 1977:[27]

As you eat breakfast you look out the window... and there's the Mediterranean area, Greece and Rome and North Africa and the Sinai. You go down across North Africa and out over the Indian Ocean and look up at that great subcontinent of India... out over the Philippines and up across the monstrous Pacific Ocean. `

---

26   *The Overview Effect,* American Institute of Aeronautics and Astronautics, Inc., Reston, VA, 1998
27   later published by Lindisfarne/Harper & Row, *Earth's Answer: Explorations of Planetary Culture,* West Stockbridge, MA, 1977

You finally come up across the coast of California, and you look for those friendly things, Los Angeles and Phoenix, and on across to El Paso. And there's Houston, there's home... and you look and sure enough, there's the Astrodome, and you identify with that, it's an attachment. And on across New Orleans and then you look down to the south, and there's the whole peninsula of Florida laid out...

The next thing you recognize in yourself is that you're identifying with North Africa: you look forward to that. You anticipate it, and there it is. That whole process of what you identify with begins to shift.

When you go around the Earth in an hour and a half, you begin to recognize that your identity is with that whole thing. That makes a change. You look down there and you can't imagine how many borders and boundaries you cross, again and again and again, and you don't even see them. There you are —hundreds of people are killing each other over some imaginary line that you're not even aware of and that you can't see.

From where you see it, the thing is a whole, and it's so beautiful. You wish you could take one in each hand, one from each side in the various conflicts, and say, 'Look. Look at it from this perspective. Look at that. What's important?'

You look down and see the surface of that globe you've lived on all this time, and you know all those people down there and they are like you, they are you—and somehow you represent them. You are up there as the sensing element, that point out on the end, and that's a humbling feeling.

It's a feeling that says you have responsibility. It's not for yourself. The eye that doesn't see doesn't do justice to the body. That's why it's there; that's why you are out here. And somehow you recognize that you're a piece of this total life.

So...that's a change. That's something new. And when you come back there's a difference in the world now. There's a difference in that relationship between you and the planet, and you and all those other forms of life on that planet, because you've had that kind of experience.

TO CAUSE TRANSFORMATION, YOU HAVE TO GIVE UP ALL ATTACHMENT TO OUTCOMES

I love results. No results, no satisfaction. No results, no bread or clothes for the kids. Results make bosses happy. Even better, they can be measured. There's nothing soft or wooly about results. Real men and women get results. Results make the world go around. Results drive the economy. If anyone says that results are a bad idea, they are shunned or dumped. There is no arguing with results.

Still, the greater one's attachment to results, the less transformation is possible, and the fewer new possibilities. The world of results is concrete and the world of imagination isn't. There's an inverse relationship between attachment to results and the capacity to create possibility, for oneself and others. Complete attachment to results requires that there is always somewhere to go to. Consequently, there is little attachment to the *moment of now* — the very presence required for transformation: a quantum leap.

This is not to knock results. But, where there is addiction to short-term, quarterly report-driven results, there is rarely transformation or unpredictable, positive futures. This might explain periodic meltdowns where people are so busy making money, buying and selling, or investing that they can neither see nor begin to transform the quicksand behind the curtain.

*The less one's attachment to outcomes, the greater
the chance of a producing a transformation.*

Transformation is an altered state — a new relationship to one's self, to someone else, to a company, or to anything. But to produce transformation consistently and reliably, you have to give up all attachment to any particular outcome. This is so counterintuitive as to sound ridiculous to anyone with a bottom line bent.

Maybe there is so little transformation because leaders get paid for results and outcomes. Transformation happens in people's minds before it can happen in the world around them. The inability to let go of outcomes and focus on what is real, true, and present, is a box that stops imagination in its tracks.

Imagination and results do not live in the same house. If you want to think completely from the future, try blocking all attachment to results.

A focus on results brings certainty. Uncertainty is a necessary mountain to be climbed. I remember a team meeting in the engineering division of a global consumer goods business. They were dedicated, competent, and cooperative, and what they said sounded concrete and intelligent. They were one hundred percent dedicated to certainty, to solving the problems at hand, designing a system that worked, and being as thorough as they could.

Yet I knew from private conversations that they had issues — with the leader, with their relationships, with morale in their own teams, and with an abiding boredom vis-à-vis the prospect of their future. It was their seamless focus on engineering content and a quest for certainty that prevented attention to anything else.

I have come to believe there is an inverse relationship between new possibility and the insistence on certainty. Many people are certainty addicts. I once asked my Gestalt teacher, Erving Polster, how he was able to stay so alive, creative, and animated. He said, *I pay more attention to my confusion than to my certainty.*

WHAT SHOULD WE STIMULATE?

What do the following have in common?

- World War Two
- the NASA Apollo Program
- the X Prize Foundation
- Campbell's Soup of Canada

In each case, winning was decisive.

Allies in each of these examples accomplished extraordinary goals involving the survival and advancement of a system or purpose they deeply cared about.

- In World War Two, we and our allies won a global war against two powerful, implacable enemies.
- In the Apollo Program, we sent men to the moon and returned them again in nine years.
- In the X Prize competition, nongovernmental organizations built and flew vessels into space in a remarkably short time, for a ten-million-dollar prize.
- In Campbell's Soup of Canada, a former client, staff, and consultants saved Canadian manufacturing from being sent to the United States.

There are many more such examples of victory. In each case, the leaders threw their hats over the wall and committed themselves and their constituents to a cause in the face of massive uncertainty, such as:

- "unconditional surrender"
- landing on the moon
- building a successful low-cost spaceship
- saving a company with economics against it

In each case, the goal was precise and required unpredictable breakthroughs in courage, imagination, technology, and management.

In each case, leaders inspired people to do what they were capable of, not just what they typically do.

In each case, collective innovation and cooperation was contagious. By whatever means — political, inspirational, financial, scientific, technical, logistical — people pulled together for the sake of the challenge and its ever-present importance.

In the movie *Field of Dreams*, long-dead players gathered to relive their past and entertain those people who could see them. Some could see them and others couldn't. As in the movie, the ideas and possibilities in this book come alive when these conditions for victory are the field of play:

- Leaders pledging themselves and their constituents to an inspired cause in the face of massive uncertainty.
- Having goals that are precise, calling for unpredictable breakthroughs in courage, imagination, technology, and management.

- Leaders inspiring people to do what they are capable of, not just what they do.
- Mobilizing contagious innovation and cooperation, *by whatever means*, with all possible support.

Given these conditions for victory, there are countless tools, resources, technologies, facilitation, and training already available. Without the field of play, these same tools just don't seem relevant.

> *The challenge is in legitimizing important*
> *cross-boundary conversations in the first place.*
> *While most people will agree that this is a good idea,*
> *few will take it on.*

However, if all of this brilliant energy never gets focused collectively, what will happen instead is endless conversation trying to satisfy individual paradigm interests. New technologies for inexpensive energy independence, clean environments, and social transformation either won't go anywhere or won't develop fast enough to make a difference.

In my work with enlisting such open-ended, cross-paradigm dialogue, I've encountered seven levels at which people engage with the opportunity. Starting with the lowest, these are:

Sabotage: People are intolerant and suppress the possibility of engaging points of view other than their own.

Avoid: People avoid dialogue and the exploration of underlying assumptions and benefits of others' points of view.

Aware: People are aware of the potential benefits of collaborating with others who have different fundamental operating beliefs, but do not do it themselves, nor ask it of others.

Participate: People participate, if asked, in "bridging" conversations with others, but do not initiate such activity.

Enroll: People ask for others' involvement in cross-paradigm conversations about fundamental points of view.

Design: People formulate plans and processes to induce, encourage, and sustain uncharacteristic conversations to find common ground and new possibilities between those who normally do not listen to one another in a serious way.

Lead: People stimulate transformational conversations that honor individual points of view and legitimize the utility of each in service of a common cause.

A simple conversation clarifies where people are, and they can be addressed accordingly. While some might move up the scale, you have to start with where they are.

The needed outcomes require working with people
at the higher ends of this scale,
as well as within the conditions for victory.

☙❧

The best thing for being sad, replied Merlin to
young King Arthur, is to learn something.
That's the only thing that never fails.

You may grow old and trembling in your anatomies,
you may lie awake at night listening to the disorder of your veins,
you may miss your only love, you may see the world about you dev-
astated by evil lunatics, or know your honour trampled in the sewers
of baser minds.

There is only one thing for it then — to learn.
Learn why the world wags and what wags it. That is the only thing
which the mind can never exhaust, never alienate, never be tortured
by, never fear or distrust, and never dream of regretting.
Learning is the only thing for you.

Look what a lot of things there are to learn — pure science, the only purity there is. You can learn astronomy in a lifetime, natural history in three, and literature in six. And then, after you have exhausted a million lifetimes in biology and medicine and criticism and geography and history and economics — why, then you can start to make a cartwheel out of the appropriate wood, or spend fifty years learning to begin to learn to beat your adversary at fencing. After that, you can start again on mathematics, until it is time to learn to plough.

T.H. White, *The Once and Future King*[28]

---

28   Berkley Medallion Books, York, *1958*

A PERSONAL NOTE

I want my children and the people I love to spend much of their time outside the box, basking in the continuing sunlight of new possibility.

I want to see navigators all over the world come out of hiding, step up to the plate, and hit home runs with the grace and power of Ted Williams in Fenway Park.

I want to see bureaucracies disappear in a sea of dialogue and co-invention, and a world in which education convinces most people that transformation is always possible.

I want everyone to see that incremental change is a lie, that real change requires a discontinuity, and everything else comes to feel like more of the same.

I want everyone to realize that there is always a moment-to-moment choice between being a victim and seeking a breakthrough.

Upon a small number of committed and humane people,
the future of the world depends.

AFTERWORD

Introducing the *Merlin Navigator* and ToolBox

The *Merlin Navigator* is a revolutionary on-line assessment tool that predicts the current chances of success for any important and ambitious goal. The prediction is based on eight critical success factors, using an algorithm drawn from more than forty years of experience working with companies and government agencies all over the world.

Here's an overview of how it works:

- An important goal is defined by a leader or project manager.
- Designated members of that team are asked to complete a 20-minute questionnaire.
- Results are immediately available, and show the project's likelihood of success, indicating specifically where the team is performing well and precisely where attention is needed to increase chances of success.

The *Merlin Navigator* has proven effective whether projects are:

- Start Ups
- Turn Arounds
- Complex Change Projects
- Mergers or Acquisions
- Business as Usual

An available option, the *Merlin Navigator Toolbox* directs users to an exhaustive set of tools, practices, processes, and information that immediately improve their chances of success.

With the *Merlin Navigator* you can obtain the quality of world-class consulting advice to address your challenges, at a fraction of the cost.

To learn more, visit www.MerlinNavigator.com.

We welcome your comments and contributions to this work.
*Contact us at **NavigatingFromTheFuture.com**.*

ABOUT THE AUTHOR

Charles E Smith, PhD has been an executive coach and organizational development consultant to senior leaders of companies, associations, and government agencies in the United States, England, and Canada since 1969. Charlie and his associates have made it possible for hundreds of businesses and government organizations to solve their most intractable problems. Leaders and their staffs utilizing his approaches have achieved seemingly impossible objectives through dramatic increases in cooperation and personal development.

Charles holds degrees from the Boston Public Latin School, Harvard College, Harvard Business School, and Case Western Reserve University, and a certificate from the Gestalt Institute of Cleveland. In addition to direct work with clients, he has served on the faculties of Sir George Williams University, the McGill University School of Education, and the McGill Centre for Management Education. Charlie was on the Board of Directors for the Foundation for Mid-East Communication and the National Peace Institute Foundation. He co-founded the Middle Road Foundation for Native American Youth in Taos, New Mexico, and is a past President of the Harvard-Radcliffe Club of New Mexico. He is currently on the Board of ATWG (the Aerospace Technology Working Group).

Charlie's first book, *The Merlin Factor: Keys to the Corporate Kingdom,* was published in 1995. In addition to white papers and conference presentations, he has published articles in the London Business School's *Strategy Review* and authored the chapter, "Stage Three Leadership: From Good Ideas to Unified Action" in *Beyond Earth: The Future of Humans in Space, 2006.*

ABOUT THE COVER

"Infinite Fields of Energy"
Oil on Wood, Velka Edge-Olok

Velka blends Andean and European traditions in multi-dimensional works, which have been exhibited at the Hong Kong Science and Technology Park, the New York Arts League, the My Moon Gallery, and 75 Greene House Soho Gallery, and in the first Outer Space Exhibit aboard the Japanese Sprite Satellite. A principal in the 2020 Art on the Moon project, sponsored by Ultra-Future World, Velka's projects focus on self-discovery and the evolution of humanity through creative, interactive art. She can be reached at: www.m2studios.us & www.FirstArtOnTheMoon.com.

◕◔

In Velka's painting I caught a glimpse of evolution. I saw the promise Thomas Paine made in the pamphlet "Common Sense *at the time of the American Revolution:* "We have it within us to begin the world over again." *I saw the Chalice and the Sword of male and female energy it will take to make a world that works for everyone who steps up to the challenge of personal responsibility. I saw the immediacy and power of a* Starry Night, *and of going to the moon. I saw the message of the book, not in words but in a panoply of color, directionality and presence.*

Charles E Smith

◕◔